"Giraffe-Neck Girl"

"Giraffe-Neck Girl"

Make Friends with Different Cultures

Jackie Chase

WorldTravelDiva.com
CulturesOfTheWorld.com

Color Edition
"Giraffe-Neck Girl"
Make Friends with Different Cultures
By Jackie Chase

AdventureTravelPress.com, Lady Lake FL 32159
© 2014 Jackie Chase
All rights reserved. Published 2014

Printed in the United States of America
Color Print: ISBN- 978-1-937630-50-8
E-book: ISBN- 978-1-937630-51-5

Library of Congress Cataloging
Travel
Library of Congress Control Number: 2014935900

WorldTravelDiva.com
CulturesOfTheWorld.com

Other Books by
Jackie Chase
Winner of Royal Palm Literary Award and Beverly Hills Book Awards

"All Hands Working Together" Cruise for a Week: Meet 79 Cultures

"How to Become An Escape Artist" A Traveler's Handbook

"100 People to Meet Before You Die" Travel to Exotic Cultures

"Walking to Woot" Mom and Teen Bond in Primitive Culture (fall, 2014)

Contents

1. Mucha playing hand games

Introduction

People say that variety is the spice of life. The world is full of unique and interesting cultures. The giraffe-necked women of the Padaung tribe appear to have the most unusual of all traditional customs.

The opportunity to wear brass neck rings for a lifetime begins for them at about four years old. The obvious discomfort and daily chore of cleaning the brass, as well as the necessity of drinking with a straw (the girls cannot tilt their heads back to empty a glass of liquid), does not trouble these tribal women; they say they are happy to carry out the tradition.

As their young lives unfold, they emerge from their chrysalis (the protective shell of a growing butterfly) into beautiful young girls, the envy of the village.

The sun begins to go down over the horizon, and the only noise comes from children playing in the dirt roads. Outside cooking areas are equipped with candles ready to light when darkness decides to hide blackened metal pots and rice sacks slumped over at the base of trees.

For ten-year-old Mucha, the sun close to the horizon means it is time to start the fire for dinner. She does not wear a watch, but she knows it has been a long day since her last meal; yes, she ate a bowl of rice while the sun woke the village.

Mucha lives in a small village in a forested valley in northern Thailand, close to the border with Myanmar.

The Padaung tribal people of Mucha's village live simple lives in small huts without electricity, toilets, or running water, and they walk around on dirt floors.

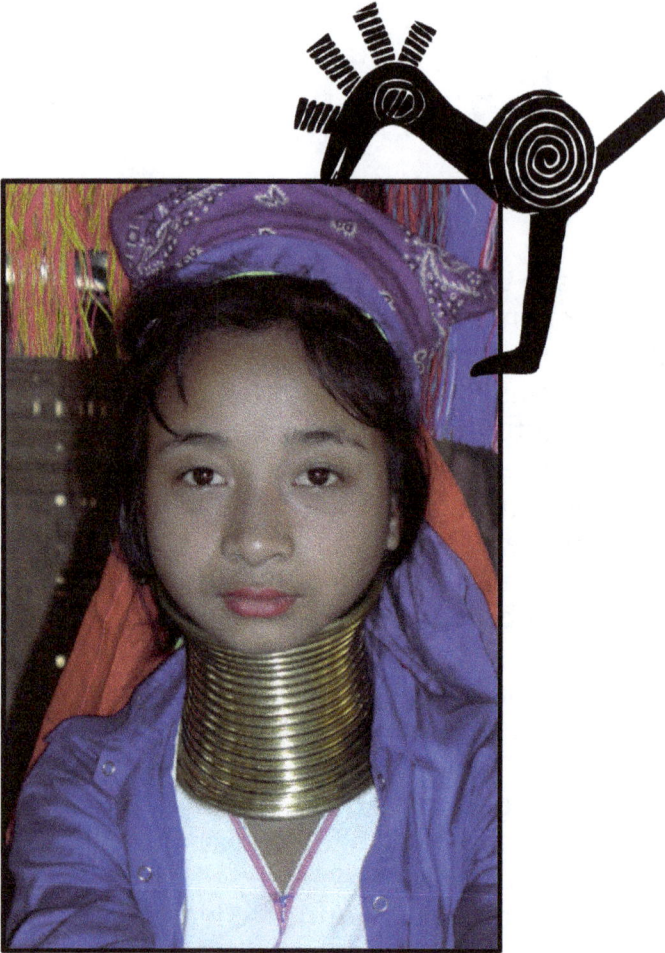

2. Teenage giraffe-neck girl

Geography of Village

Mucha's village, called Ban Nai Soi, stretches up and down dusty rutted roads. Bamboo huts with thatched roofs provide shelter for over 235 people (or about 40 families).

The forty kilometer (24 miles) between Mae Hong Son (sometimes called the Switzerland of Thailand) and Mucha's village is studded with rocks and pitted with holes.

3. Typical village hut

The motorcyclists who will take you on that journey can do it in less than an hour.

Being so close to the Myanmar border, Mae Hong Son sits between the competing powers of the Myanmar government (formerly called Burma) and the Thai government.

The influence of Burmese culture can be seen everywhere, especially in the architecture of the monasteries. A picture perfect example of the temple architecture is the Wat John Kham.

Homes

The village of Ban Nai Soi consists of approximately forty wood houses, all with thatched leaf roofs. Each house has two or three rooms with dirt floors. Some of the houses have sheets of linoleum, usually a bright

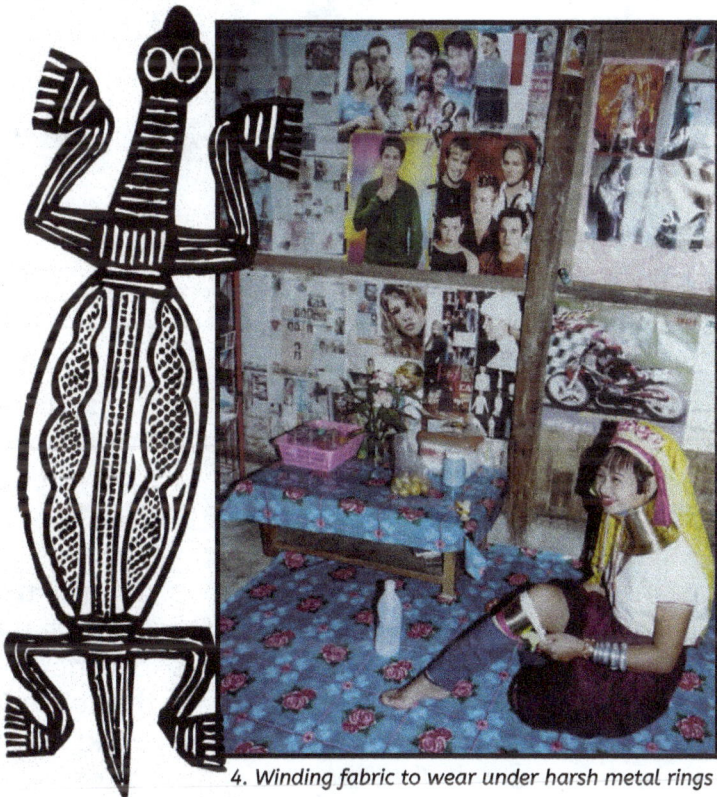

4. Winding fabric to wear under harsh metal rings

color like red or blue, to cover the floor of the main living room area. The walls have posters from old movies or favorite actors or actresses, or very old calendars and pages from newspapers. If a tourist was kind enough to send back photos she took of these people, one might see a photo of the family or one of the family members displayed on the wall as well. A Ban Nai Soi house might have a wood shelf with inexpensive figurines from China or Taiwan decorating it, and maybe even a plastic vase filled with artificial flowers covered in dust.

5. Mucha's house

The coconut palm leaf is used for the roofs. It takes several men to gather leaves and rebuild a neighbor's roof. Often small repairs to a hole in a roof will keep a father busy.

A thatched roof made of coconut palm leaves lasts about four to five years before needing repairs, using techniques from centuries past. Pieces of the coconut palm leaf are soaked in water for several days to remove any insects that might cause further damage to the house. The leaves are then beaten flat to soften them, and washed again in clear water before they are set out to dry.

4

Play

The playtime activities of the children of Ban Nai Soi focus around nature and each other. They love playing, singing, and running, but it all involves using their imagination. Their games involve no toys, computers, or hand-held electronics.

6. Young Karen tribal girl

A group of boys, about ten to twelve years old, plays soccer using a wadded piece of newspaper for their ball. They do not seem to mind, as it probably feels much better on their bare feet than a normal soccer ball.

Small groups of children, usually very young, busy themselves under tall trees, always looking up. They will take a tree branch, about ten feet long, and pull back the bark to form a thin pointed end. They will cover the end with a black sticky sap and listen as they walk. When they hear a locust or cicada, they will look into the trees and, after finding it, touch the insect with the sticky end of the branch.

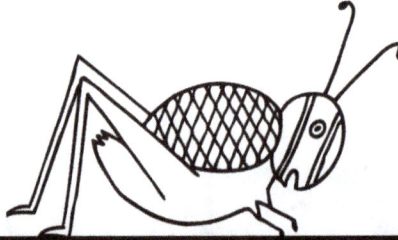

7. Catching locusts with bamboo pole

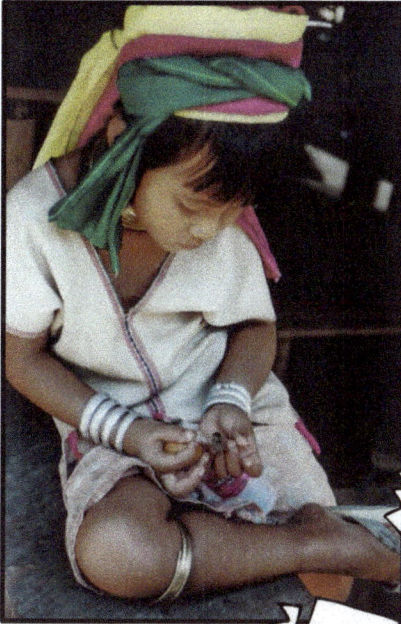

8. Playing with locust
before eating it raw

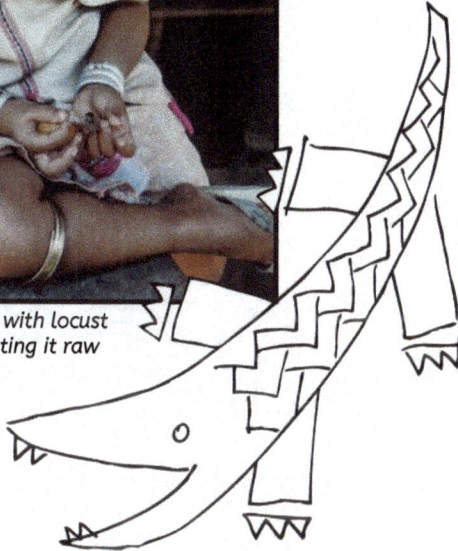

The insect will buzz like crazy trying to get free, but even the littlest of children (perhaps only three years old) will take the bug off the sticky branch and play with it for a few minutes. They might pass it back and forth to other friends, laughing at the buzzing insect, but eventually they'll pull its wings off and plop it into one of their mouths for an afternoon snack! Carefree and still hungry, one or two children will grab the sticks and head once more for the tree-lined ditches, humming a song while looking for more locusts.

9. Playing hopscotch

Hopscotch is another favorite game played, with squares drawn in the dirt with sticks. Groups of children, large or small, will sit on porches waiting their turn to throw the rock and hop through the course.

8

Walking through the village, a tourist might have the opportunity to see a small group of children playing jump rope. There are no stores for shopping, and creativity is a huge part of growing up with nature's products. Vines or very thin strips of bamboo make perfect ropes for jumping.

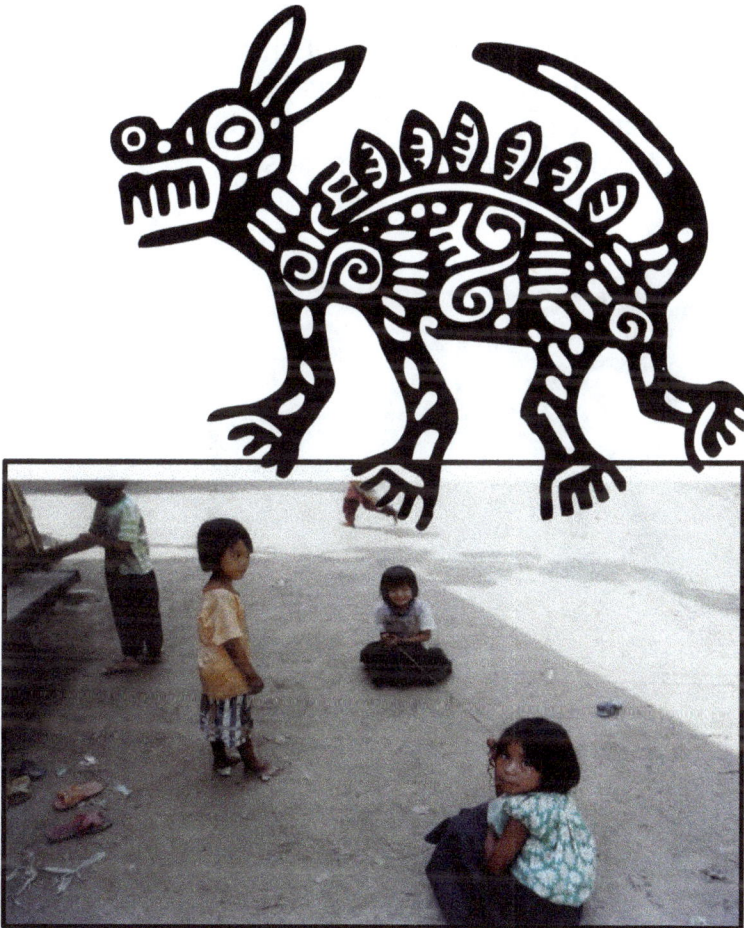

10. Jump rope with rubber bands tied into rope

Imagination turns a puddle of water into a lake for huge make-believe sailing ships that float around with seeds for people and grains of rice for cargo. Perhaps a tourist at one time showed the village children pictures of boats, or maybe they discovered that a thin piece of wood or a leaf would float. An old rusty piece of wire bent in the shape of a bridge makes for a perfect crossing for motorbikes made of chips of bark.

One of Mucha's favorite pastimes is making mud pies and fancy mud cakes out of mud, sand, and little scraps of twigs, flowers, and seeds.

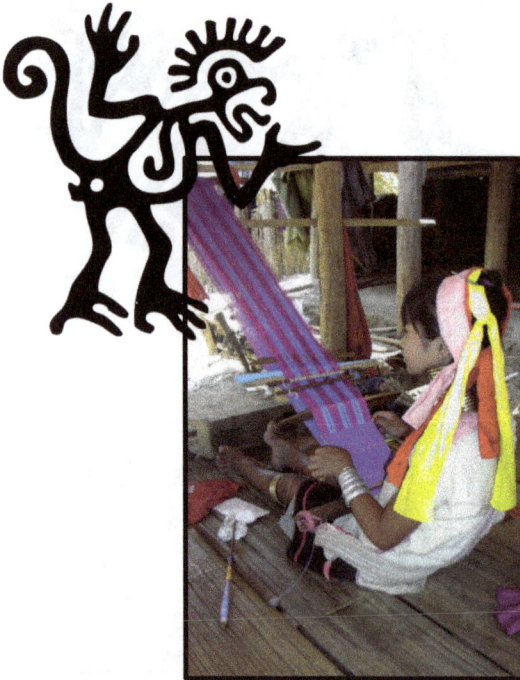

11. Back strap weaving

An empty tin can Mucha finds in the trash of a tiny little shop within their village makes a vase for tiny flower petals.

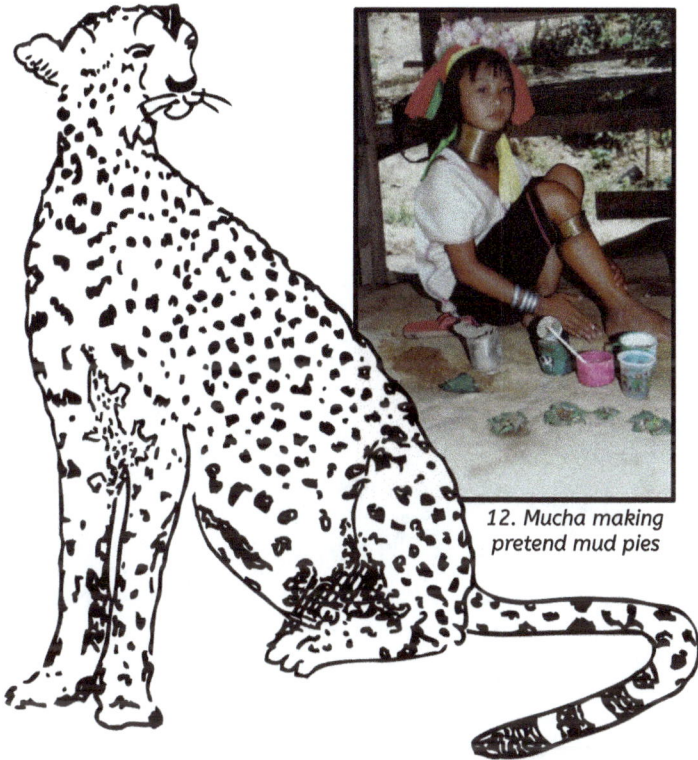

12. Mucha making pretend mud pies

The afternoon heat provides a reason for Mucha's mother to nap with Mucha's younger brother Suracha. Mucha sits under the family table of souvenirs for protection from the sun, singing and tending to her mud garden. Her brother loves to sneak away from naptime and help Mucha with her decorations.

School

Filled with dust from the dirt floors, the Padaung School occupies a small corner at the edge of the village. Huge windows on three sides join the open front section of the school building, allowing relief from the hot sun. On the back wall, a large blackboard hangs facing a few wood desks about the width of four children each.

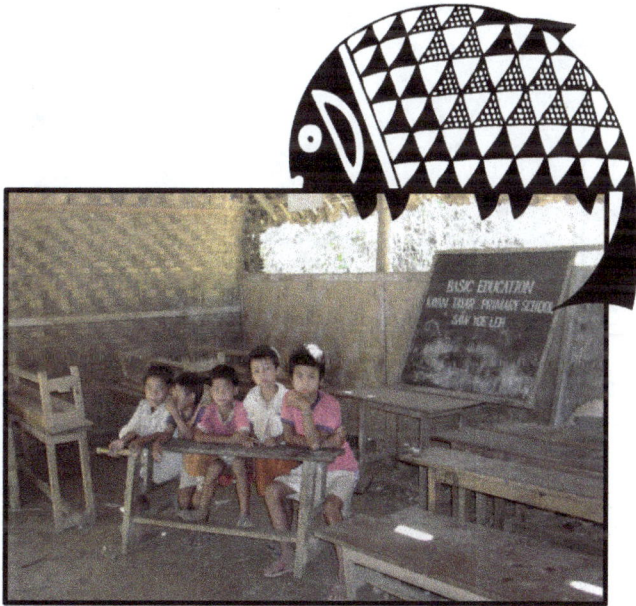

13. Boys in school classroom

There are no books, paper or pencils, anywhere in the room. The Padaung children go to school if the parents can afford for them to leave home for a few hours each day. Some children stay at home to help with watching younger brothers or sisters while parents work in fields or weave articles to sell to tourists.

The school session lasts for nine months of the year, similar to schools in the United States, with summer months off being April, May, and June. The children attend school for three to five years while learning math, reading, and writing plus four languages: Karen, English, Thai, and Burmese.

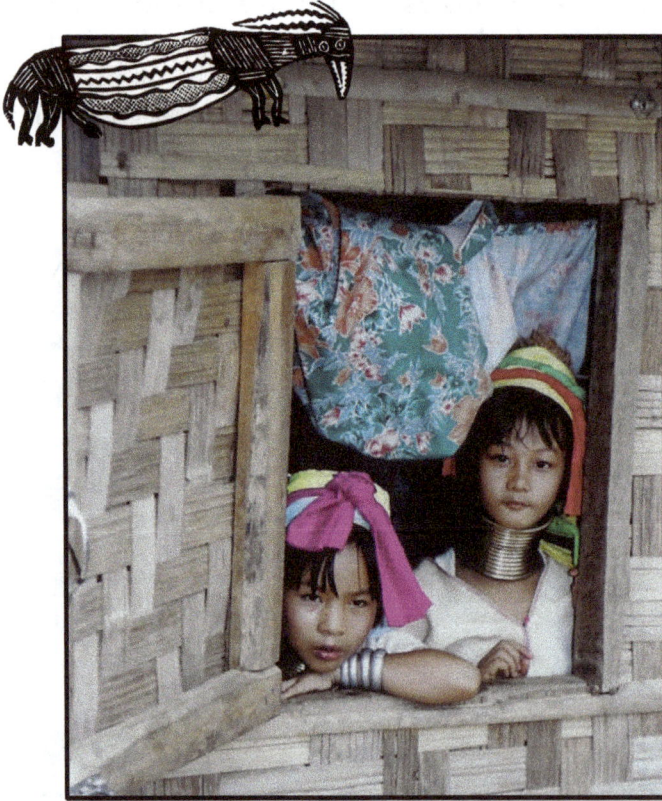

14. Watching neighbors play from window

If they want to continue on to high school, there are volunteer teachers in the refugee camp behind their village. It was reported that four girls were about to graduate from high school and come back to the Padaung village to teach. For the girls who wear the brass neck rings, there is no hope of leaving the village and pursuing a career in the outside world. The Thai government does not pay any money to the Padaung for education.

A teacher from the Padaung village of Huay Puu Kaeng says, "The children have difficulties learning how to read and write since their own language has no written form....I don't know what the future holds for them....The girls will end up doing what their mothers are doing."

15. Girls in classroom

16. Roasting a pig over a fire

16

Food and Grocery Shopping

The main staple of food for the Padaung is rice. Mucha is old enough to help prepare the evening meal, starting with building a fire for the cooking of the rice. After she builds the fire, her mother prepares the rice and adds vegetables as it cooks. Another fire is used to heat water for tea that has been grown in nearby villages. Some of the families are lucky enough to raise pigs. Walking down the alleyways of the village, one might see several men preparing a fire, killing a pig and cooking it. After roasting the pig and scraping the singed hair away, men skin the pig and delivered it to the elders. The elders of each family share in the process of cutting the meat and equally dividing it.

Because there is no electricity in their village, the families have no method to keep food fresh. The villagers use the sun as their oven to dry meat. Dried meat lasts for long periods without the need for refrigeration. The only kind of milk available is powdered, and this is mixed with river water.

A small pickup truck manages the rutted narrow roads once a week. Fresh fish, eggs, vegetables, and fruits fill divided cubicles in the back. Mucha's eyes light up when she hears the truck arrive. Her mother suggests she pick a few tangerines while she watches the live ducks covered with nets and quacking for their freedom.

The fish she has chosen for a special meal smells, and Mucha makes a funny face while carrying it back to her home's cooking area. Outside the family's hut sits the kitchen area; it includes a fire pit for cooking, and piles of metal pots, lids, and metal plates. No silverware is used at meals.

The Padaung do not own large plots of land for farming rice or tea, the two crops grown in the area where they live.

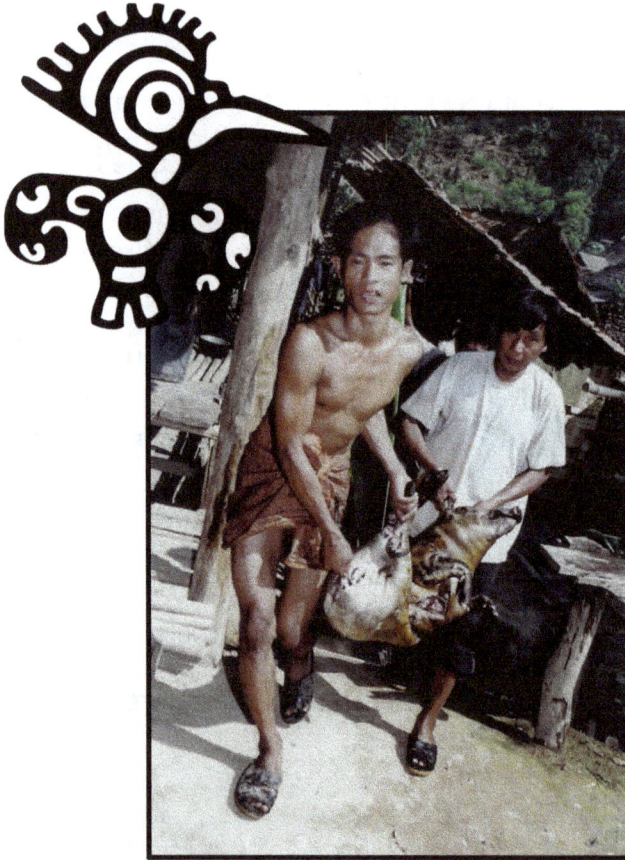

17. Carrying a cooked pig

Government organizations like the International Rescue Committee donate rice to refugee camps like Ban Nai Soi.

The water supply for Ban Nai Soi comes from the river in a hose system running throughout the village. Water is stored in large cement tanks about five feet in diameter and about two feet deep. The water is always ice-cold river water. Without electricity in the village, the residents rely on candles for light.

18. Mucha choosing a duck for dinner

Chores

In the village of Padaung, the men live a much easier life than the women, who wear the brass rings while working. Some of the families have small pieces of land to farm, giving them a place to grow a few vegetables. Some of the men spend time cutting wood for cooking fires with their sons, and gather small branches for kindling. A father's free time might include swinging in hammocks, smoking hand-made cigars, and sipping rice beer.

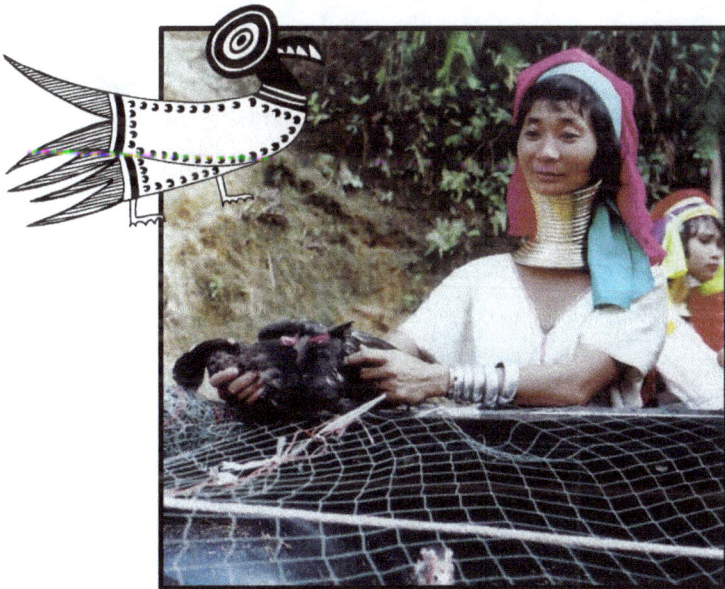

19. Showing ducks to Mucha

Mucha's father, Ladu, spent several days building a cement walkway in front of his house.

The village water tank located in front of Ladu's house created a muddy mess. He sectioned off a small area for a walkway and prepared it for the cement.

His wife, Matu, and a neighbor lady both dug dirt from an area beyond his house and carried it to the new section in small buckets for hours and hours.

Ladu mixed the dirt and sand with cement and, by hand, troweled it into the new section while the women carried more and more sand and dirt, as he needed it. Not many men appear outside during a daytime walk through the village.

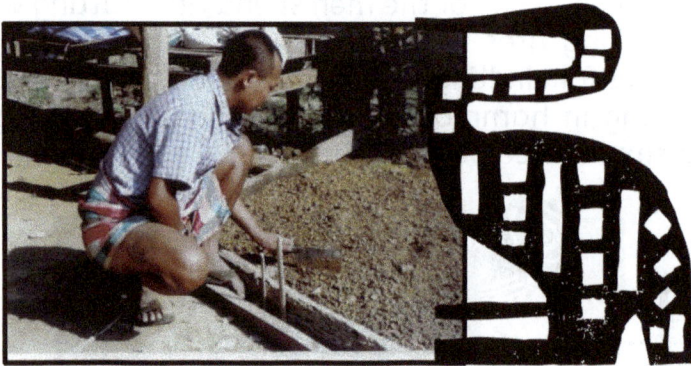

20. Mucha's father building a cement walkway

The Padaung women work hard at keeping their homes clean and their children busy.

A woman's day starts with sweeping the house clean of all loose dust covering the hard-packed dirt floor.

A small dish of rice gives each family member enough energy to get through the day. After breakfast cleanup, the women settle into a weaving routine outside their homes in the shade of shelters made of bamboo.

Ledges in the shelters provide work areas or places for the women to nap. A long table might be set up in front of one of these shelters and covered with souvenirs to sell to tourists passing by.

Homemade jewelry and long woven scarves or shawls, plus some postcards and other inexpensive

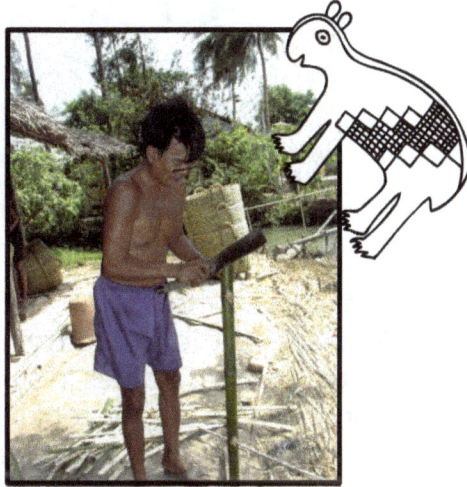
21. Cutting bamboo

crafts, are available for sale, one toppling over one another on the table. A handmade guitar or other musical instrument might gather dust on some tables. Families sell crafts made in factories, earning commissions on each item sold.

One such item is a wooden rice pot, made for carrying and storing rice. The pot has beautiful hand-painted tribal scenes decorating its sides.

Children, sometimes only four or five years old, manage the tables until tourists appear.

They will then call to alert their mothers about a potential sale.

Often during the day, children build pretend villages with mounds of sand under family tables, safe from the sun.

Families trade their woven pieces for items they need, like clothing and food. Unlike people in devel-

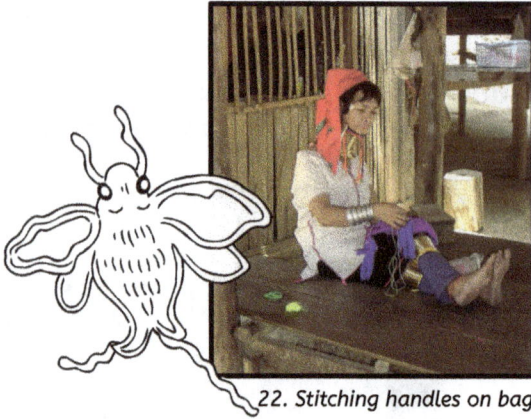

22. Stitching handles on bag

oped nations, the Padaung are uncomfortable working for money. Men spend their time trying to repair their houses, growing a few vegetables in small gardens, and occasionally preparing a pig for cooking. Tourists come to the village offering small amounts of cash for the individual families to use for the groceries they need to buy from the once-weekly food truck.

23. Padaung man selling bow and arrow

Cleaning is a daily chore for the entire family to help keep rodents (like mice and insects) out of the house. Several times a day, handmade brooms sweep the living areas.

24

Garbage or leftover food attracts insects and rodents. The family members help with sweeping, washing dishes, and washing clothes. Even the youngest of children are respon-sible for carrying a bucket of water from the village water supply tank, or filling buckets with water from one of the many blue hoses coming from the river.

Two boys about two or three years old try their best to fill their bucket with water. They keep spraying each other with the hose, and never quite figure out how to

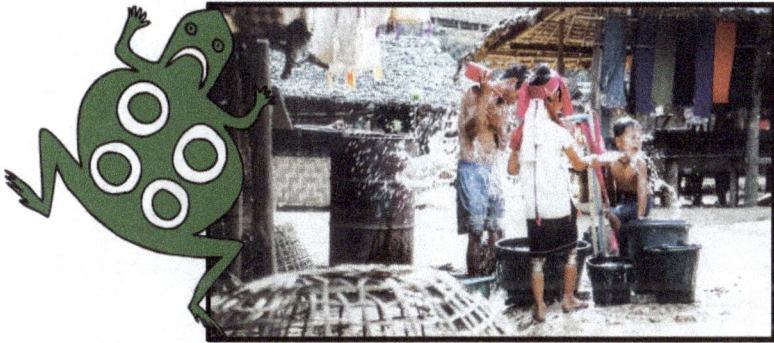

24. Cooling off at the well before dinner

get the bucket at the right level for carrying. At first, the bucket is too full and they cannot lift it. As they walk along, trying to carry it, most of the water splashes out, and by the time they manage to get halfway to their home, most of the water is gone.

25. Naptime

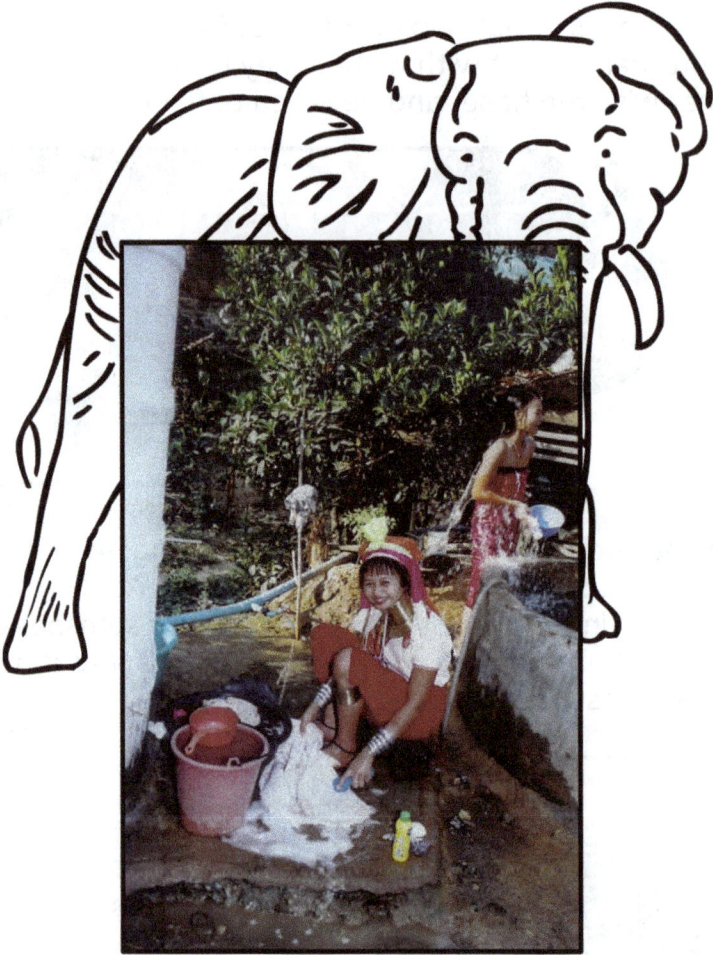

26. Washing clothes at the well

Clothing and Laundry

Mucha and Ma-Da both wear black hand-woven sarongs with hand woven white tops, like all the women of the Padaung village. It is very common for all individuals of a tribe, especially women and their daughters, to wear the same types of clothing. Western societies have influenced most indigenous peoples with western types of clothing all over the world.

Male teenagers wearing blue jeans and tee shirts are a common sight everywhere one travels, even in the more remote villages of Africa or Asia.

Much of the clothing the Padaung boys wear comes from missionaries or world organizations like the United Nations. Families may have only two pieces of clothing for each child, which makes washing clothes an everyday chore. Clothing passed down to younger children, when outgrown by older siblings, shows signs of holes from repeated washings.

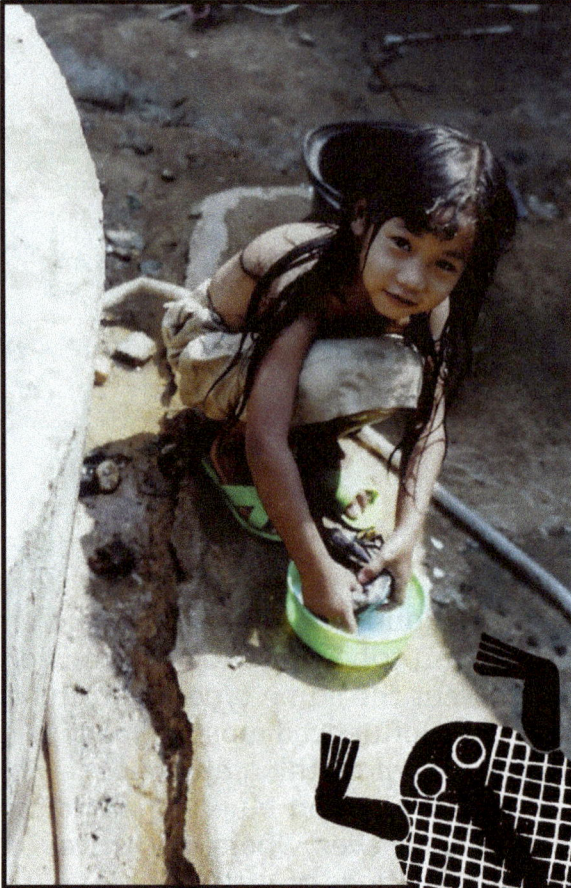

27. Three-year-old Washing her own
clothing

After soaking the fabric, individuals beat the clothing,
using sticks or stones. Matu washes clothes in a black
bucket full of soap, and rinses them in another bucket
of clear water. Matu is lucky, as the community water
supply is located in front of her house. Other families

28. Mucha's mom washing clothes in
buckets

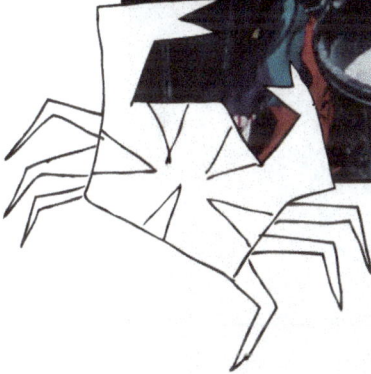

spend many hours daily just carrying water for drinking,
food preparation, and laundry to their homes.

Villagers trade for food, craft supplies, some clothing,
but not shoes. Bare feet or flip-flops make a better
alternative.

29

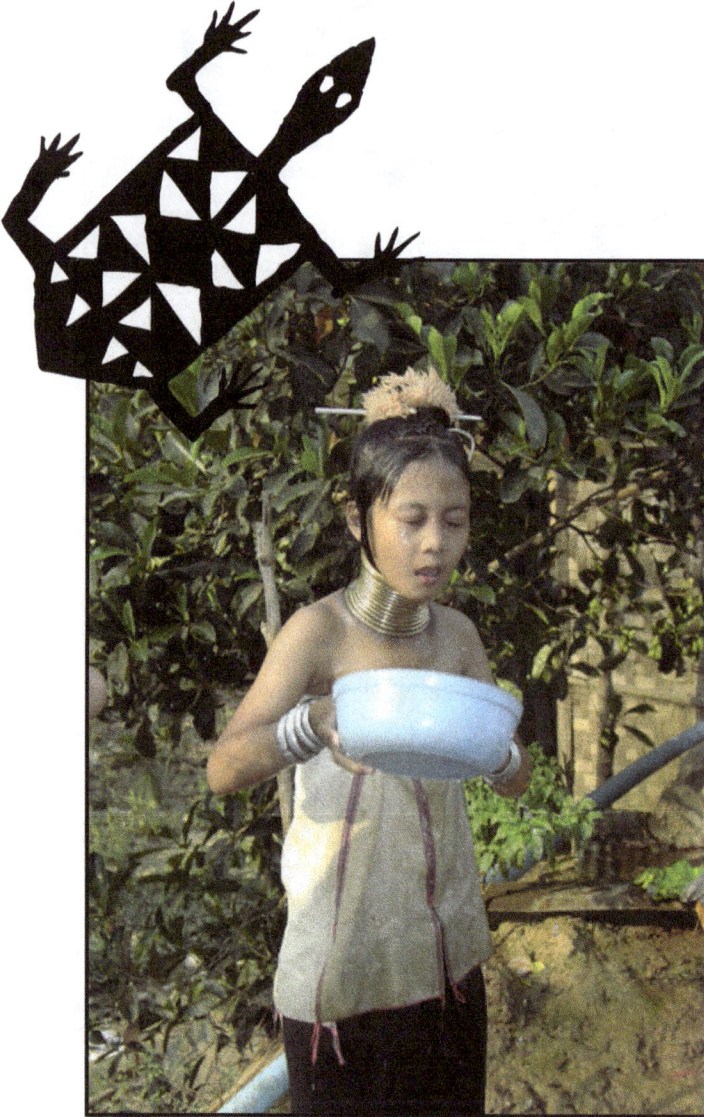

29. Mucha's bath time at the well

Bathing

For the adults of the village, bath time is a necessary daily routine to keep healthy. For the children, it is a time to cool down from the long hot day, and play in the water with friends.

Every evening at about five o'clock, children take their time weaving around houses and trees on their way to the water tank for buckets of water. They will take these back to their homes for bathing. The many blue water hoses that come from the river bring much needed water to the higher places in Nai Soi, places that are too far from the community water tank to walk for water.

30. Friends scrubbing neck rings at bath time

For the females wearing the brass rings, part of bath time is a serious time-consuming matter spent scrubbing their rings.

32

31. Scrubbing brass rings

Silver stainless steel pads, similar to those used years ago for scrubbing cast iron skillets, wash and polish the rings inside and out. Some of the women, who cannot afford to buy a stainless scrubbing pad, simply use rice straw as an abrasive tool and lime powder as a cleaner.

33

34

Family

The success of family life depends on each member contributing.

Villagers marry only members of their village. Children are very happy, and have the freedom to wander the village finding other children for playtime.

Toys, television, and computer games do not exist.

All family members share the responsibility for cooking, cleaning, laundry, and even making mud pies.

32. Mucha's family

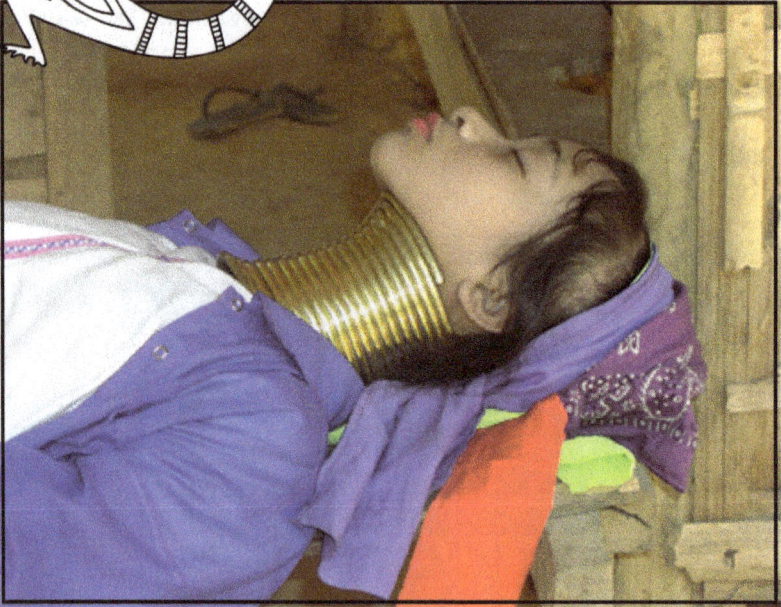

33. Sleeping with rings

Sleeping

Without air conditioning and fans to keep cool, the villagers rest in the afternoons. This time of rest is similar to siesta time in many cultures. The intense heat makes it difficult to work.

Nighttime sleeping consists of lying down on woven palm leaf mats with no blankets or pillows. The long necked women have to sleep with their heads elevated on a wooden pillow. They do not take their brass rings off ever, not even at night.

Because of the rings, they cannot lay their heads down on a flat surface. The brass rings allow a girl to turn her head from side to side but not tilt her head backwards to lie down.

The wood pillow is a wood box or wood stool about six inches off the ground. It has no padding and is just wide enough for the head. The wood stand keeps the head in a similar position like sitting or standing. If resting In a hammock, which is vertical, a woman with neck rings can relax more comfortably.

Friends

The children have many friends within the village. Neighbors and friends help each other with chores that require more than one person. You will remember when Ladu, Mucha's father, was working on the cement walkway in front of his house, the woman living next door came over and helped Matu, his wife, carry sand for the cement.

34. Children playing

Snacks

Ban Nai Soi village has a small grocery store about the size of a small bathroom with just a storefront window so customers can view the contents. The store is mostly for tourists to buy candy, cigarettes, film, and sodas. Soda pop is very popular in third and fourth world countries. It comes in glass bottles with a deposit on the glass bottle. People may also have the soda put in a plastic bag tied with a knot at the top with a straw sticking out.

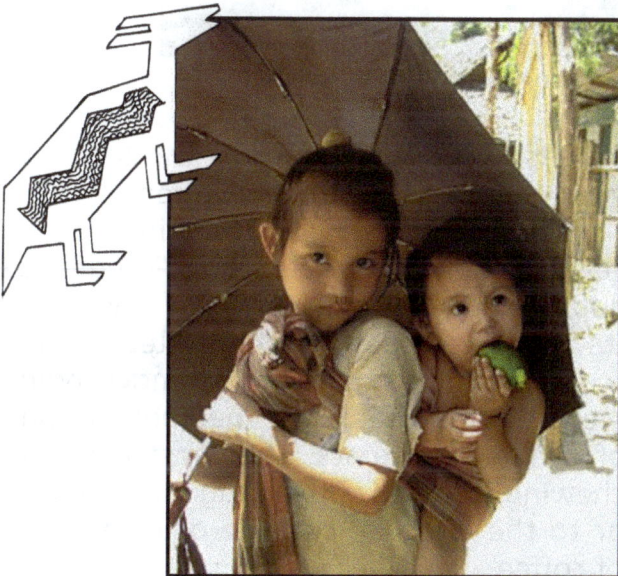

35. Babysitting baby brother

Often the villagers take the money they make from selling crafts, and walk over to the little store to buy either candy or a soda. In the middle of the afternoon, it is common to see a group of children sharing a sack of candy, or a mother sitting on the porch of the store sipping a warm soda. After the weekly visit from the grocery store truck, children enjoy tangerines and apples, a rare treat.

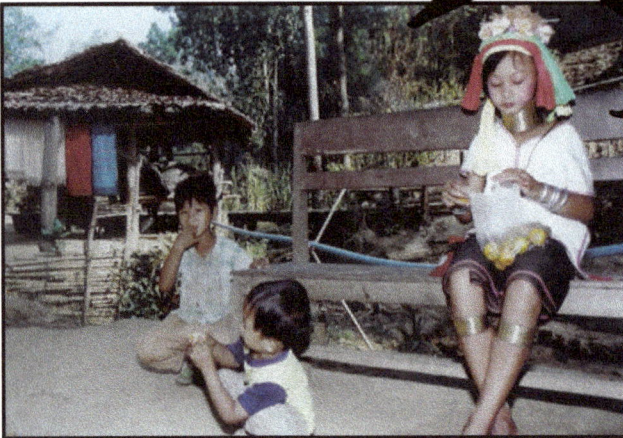

36. Snack time for Mucha and her brothers

A free and easily available snack is the locust or cicada caught in the trees by village children.

The betel nut or *Areca catechu* is a favorite chewing snack for adults. Millions of people from Vietnam, Sri Lanka, Cambodia, Indonesia, and Malaysia harvest and chew the nuts of the tropical palm tree called *Palmae*.

Other uses include treatment for stomach pains, headaches, venereal disease, fever, rheumatism, and a number of other complaints. The most common reason for chewing this nut is the drug-like affect it gives, similar to the effect of caffeine after drinking many cups of coffee.

42

In addition, the betel nut has a very bitter and sharp taste. The trees grow in moist ground and produce clusters of green fleshy nuts, which mature into yellow, and then brown, hard nuts.

Lime powder adds an even stronger flavor to betel nuts. Burning coral in an intense hot fire for several days creates lime, a white alkaline powder residue. While chewing the betel nut, a villager might take a pinch of lime powder and chew it with the nut.

Archeological studies have shown that structural and elemental changes occur in the enamel of betel-stained teeth. However, the chewing causes horrible black stains. The teeth begin to deteriorate more rapidly from chewing.

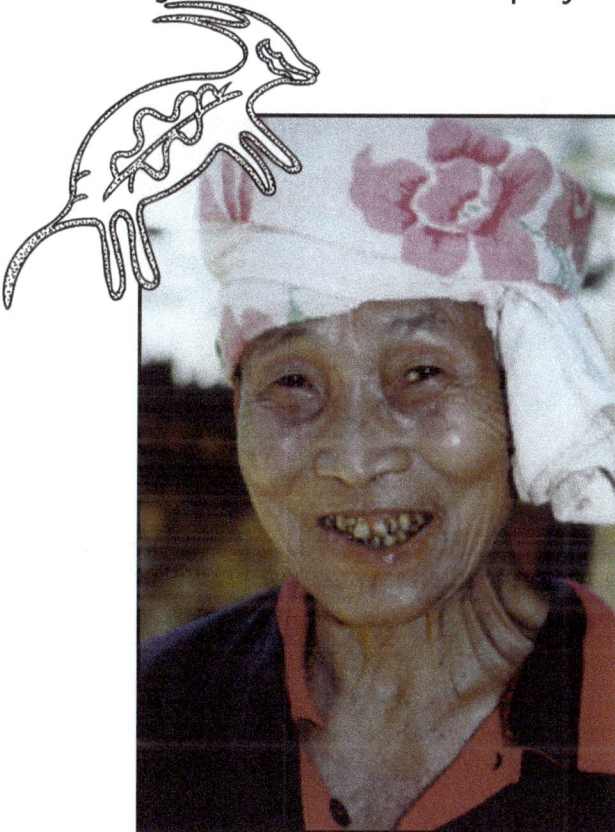

37. Stained teeth from chewing betel nuts

The gums become black and only tiny stumps remain after years and years of chewing betel nuts.

Indigenous peoples have been chewing betel nuts, sprinkled with lime powder and wrapped in Piper betel leaf, for thousands of years as evidenced by archeology. When asked why they chew the nut alone or with additives, the people cannot explain why. This age-old tradition links the Padaung with past lifestyles, and the people do not question why.

Brass Rings

Only females wear the brass neck rings. Between three and five years old, the little girls decide whether they will wear the brass rings, every day, for the rest of their lives.

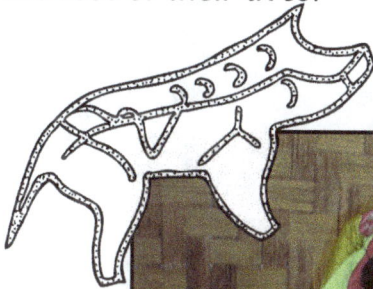

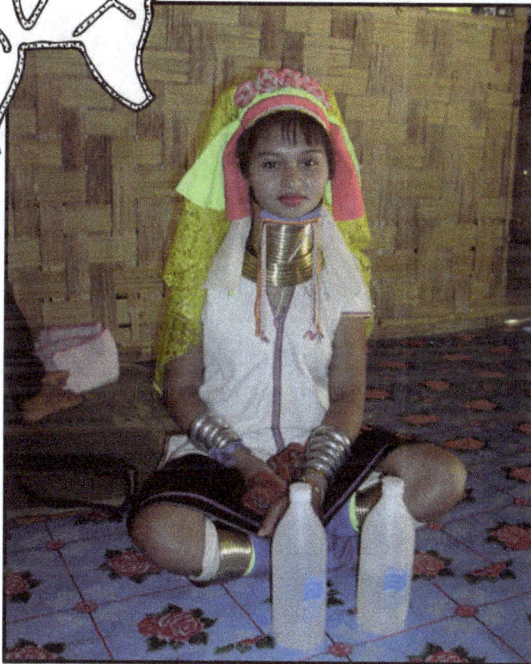

38. Ma' Da in her house

Some girls make the decision against wearing the rings. If there are older sisters and a mother wearing the rings, then there will be less financial pressure placed upon the girls to wear the rings.

Wearing the rings in today's society brings money to the family because tourists pay for photographs. Some families cannot afford to buy the rings for a younger girl. The initiation, which starts when the girls are as young as three years old, is not the beginning of womanhood nor does it involve any religious ceremony. It is just a decision made by the girls themselves.

39. Ma' Da is Mucha's teenage friend

In Myanmar/Burma, a *shaman* performs this cere-monial task. His job is to recite rituals. A Padaung man makes a brass ring resembling a large spiral coil.

A skilled, older Padaung woman then coils the ring around the child's neck. The brass ring can weigh as much as three kilos, or six and one half pounds. It looks easy to place the coil but it takes two to three hours to fit it to the neck. This art continues from generation to generation from the Padaung's ancestors. This coil will look like four or five separate rings.

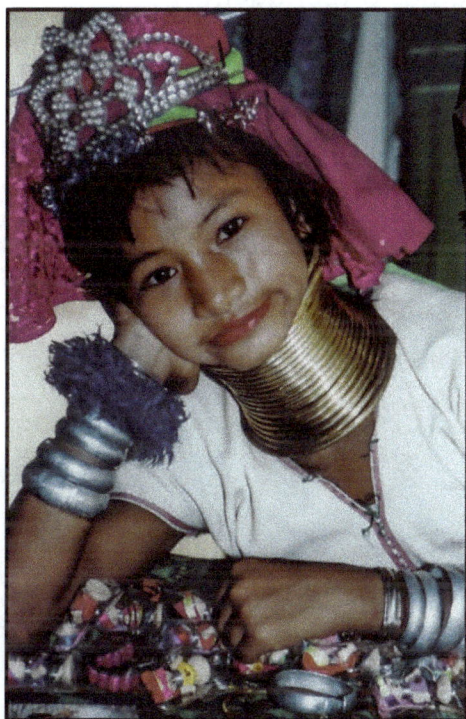

40. Trying to sell jewelry

The quantity of visual rings (in reality, the length of the brass coil) increases every year according to the age of the girl. In the beginning, the rings bruise a girl's shoulders.

When one looks closely, one can see padding under the chin to relieve the stress of the rings on the chin. As the girl outgrows the coil, a new one, which is longer and heavier, is put on until the girl reaches the age of about sixteen.

At that time, the young woman's neck looks like it has anywhere from 18 to 24 rings around it. The coil can weigh up to twenty-two kilograms, or over forty pounds. Each year, they add one or two more coil-turns (or visual rings) until the rings are fastened for life when the girl becomes a teenager.

If a four-year-old wants the rings removed within a couple of years after having them put on, her mother will remove them. The Padaungs think the rings lengthen their necks, giving them a more beautiful appearance.

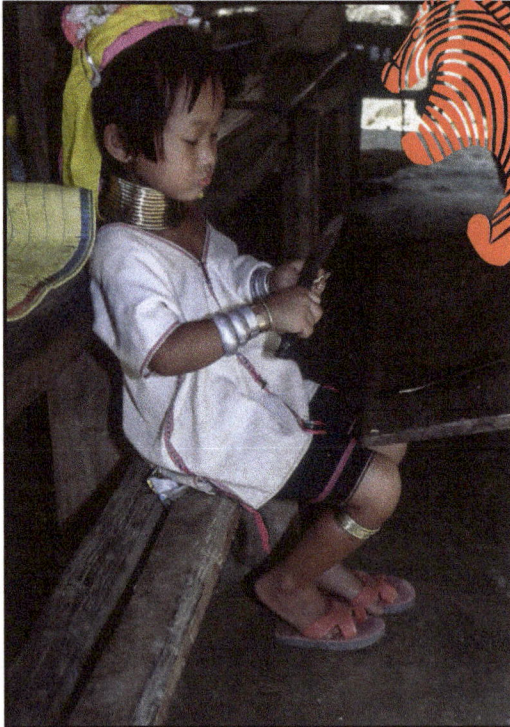

41. Four-year-old carving bamboo with knife

48

The pushed-up chin gives the elegant impression of a very tiny head floating on a golden flower stem. The reality is that the appearance of a longer neck is a visual illusion.

After many years of wearing the rings, the weight of the rings will push down and deform the collarbone and the upper ribs to such an extent that the collarbone will appear to be part of the neck.

42. *Weaving on a back strap loom*

Johan Van Rockeghem, a researcher who lived with the Padaung for six months and who speaks their language, did some extensive research on the physical impact of the brass rings. He was present when a 43-year-old Padaung woman received x-rays in a hospital in Mae Hong Son to find if there was physical damage done to her skeleton after wearing the rings for 38 years.

Many people had claimed that the brass rings would stretch the vertebrae and, in turn, lengthen the neck. Van Rockeghem stated that this would lead to eventual paralysis for the wearer. Some say the removal of the rings would cause the neck to collapse, as the muscles would have become too weak over the years to carry the weight of the head.

A normal woman's ribs grow almost horizontal, while those of the Padaung woman hang down at a 45-degree angle. The spiral brass rings were thought to rest on the collarbone, but in fact, it turns out they rest on the ribs.

The constant weight of the brass coil, and the tension between the head and the shoulders, causes pressure on the ribs. The ribs, connected to the vertebrae by a hinge joint, give way under the weight of the heavy brass spirals. The movement of the ribs drags the muscles of the shoulders down, which gives the impression of a longer neck.

The muscles move back into their normal position after removal of the brass rings, leaving the drooping ribs the only damage to the skeleton. As you can see, the length of the neck is only an illusion!

Despite the obvious discomfort, the Padaung women say they are used to the tradition of wearing the rings and are happy to continue their tribe's custom. The women do not mind putting up with the occasional discomfort of sores from the rubbing of the rings. They assume they will die with the rings still attached.

In addition to the neck rings, they wear brass rings around their wrists and calves. The women have the daily task of cleaning the rings with stainless steel pads much like our mothers used to use for cleaning pots and pans.

They use a handmade soap, lots of water, and scrub the rings, separating them as they scrub, in an attempt

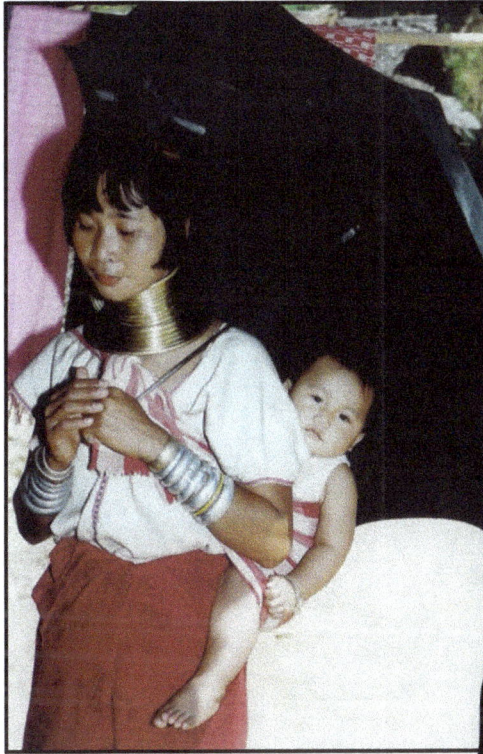

43. *Padaung mother shading her baby*

to get the rings clean on the inside as well.

It is very difficult for these women to tilt their heads back to drink, and using a straw is very common.

They live somewhat of an ordinary life: they can marry and have children, and they are able to cook, do light cleaning, and make handmade clothing from weaving on back strap looms.

Fewer than half of the hill tribe girls will start the process of wearing the rings today. The custom is slowing dying out in Thailand and in Myanmar/Burma.

The government considers the custom cruel and outlaws this extreme practice. The women of Myanmar/ Burma work hard in the fields all day and carry heavy loads of crops to and from their villages.

44. Karen woman buying snacks from girls

The neck rings are heavy and cause the woman to get tired faster plus it is difficult to carry home fire wood or crops wearing the rings.

The popularity of wearing the rings is changing. According to the Guinness Book of World Records, the maximum neck extension by the constant wearing of the brass coils is 40cm or a little more than fifteen inches.

The origin of the ring-wearing ritual among the Padaung hill tribes remains unclear.

The mythology of the Burmese PaLong tribes says that the mother of all Palong peoples was half-dragon and half-woman.

She had a beautiful long neck, and so the custom of applying neck rings to young girls was in honor to their mother-dragon. Some say the rings were to represent the humps on the dragon's back.

Other legends say that tigers only bite on the neck to kill their victims for food, so to keep the tigers from biting their necks (or, as the myths reported, to keep the lions from biting off their heads as they worked the fields and walked through the jungles each day), the women wore the rings on their necks.

A third legend of the brass rings suggested the Burmese men wanted to make their women look unattractive so that the other tribes would not capture their women and sell them as slaves.

The fourth legend reported for wearing the neck rings focused on the beauty the extra-long neck gave the woman. The women who wore the expensive rings

45. Five-year-old longneck girl

had a better chance of attracting more men from which to select husbands.

Today, one reason the women offer for wanting the brass rings is the status symbol they give. It is like wearing your bank account on your neck as those indigenous tribes of India and Africa do. Indian and African women wear heavy pieces of gold around their necks and ears, showing off the family wealth.

A 74-year-old woman, who has been wearing the rings since her fifth birthday, was asked why she wanted the rings on her neck.

She responded, "It is our tradition. About forty years ago the women stopped wearing the rings, but now they are wearing them again."

A very persistent myth about the long-necked women is that, if they were to take their brass neck rings off, their necks would collapse because their neck and shoulder muscles have weakened too much to support their heads.

As previously mentioned, X-rays, interviews of native women in their local languages, and research has confirmed that this is not true. It does take about three or four years for the muscles to return to their normal position, but no woman has yet to experience her neck collapsing.

The rings women coil around their arms and legs are similar to the neck rings. If the family cannot afford the brass or silver for arm and leg rings, they use bamboo cane.

The rings on the arms fit tightly, and begin with smaller rings at the wrists and ankles.

Padded strips of fabric protect the leg bands from rubbing and bruising the legs while the wearer walks or moves about.

History

The townspeople of Mae Hong Son are mostly of the Shan ethnic group or tribe, however various hill tribes are scattered throughout the province including Karen, Lisu, and Lahu.

Mucha belongs to a tribe called the Padaung, sometimes spelled PaDong, and often the females are called the long-necked women or giraffe women.

46. Typical village home

The Padaung tribe is a small minority of the Red Karen tribe, also called Karenni. The Red Karens used to live in Burma as a small independent state, having a private army and government. The Red Karens migrated from Mongolia, maintaining their traditional language.

In Myanmar, the Padaungs are agriculturists and hunters, being a rural race. The methods they use of farming and cultivation are desperately in need of modernization. Terrace farming, fertilization, and multiple cropping would uplift their living standards.

They produce corn, rice, cotton, pumpkins, peas, beans, ginger, tobacco, bananas, and sugarcane in quantities sufficient for their own lives. Because of Christian missionaries in the area of the Padaungs, some have embraced Christianity, but most are still Buddhists.

When the Red Karens left Burma for Thailand about twenty years ago, they took some Padaungs with them, probably thinking they could make some money from tourists wanting to see them.

Repression, poverty, and abuses by Myanmar's military rule drove the Padaungs to Thailand. The Padaung's homeland was the Kayah state in eastern Myanmar/Burma. According to a 1931 census, the Padaung population was about 16,000 in Burma. Government officials now believe the population in Myanmar/Burma is about 40,000, of which most are the "short-necked Padaung" who do not wear the neck rings.

As time has passed, more and more Padaungs have left Burma to seek refuge in Thailand, and there are now three Padaung villages close to Mae Hong Son.

The three villages have about 485 people living in them total. About three thousand people live in a refugee camp behind the village of Ban Nai Soi.

Most of the families are Karenni and the Thai government allows them to keep their own army.

Summary

This and other books in the series introduce young readers to threatened cultures and endangered peoples from different parts of the world.

47. Author with long-neck child

Presently, cultures and tribes all over the world are striving to maintain their traditional way of life, and, in some cases that are extreme, even their existence.

The entrance fee to visit the village of Ban Nai Soi supports the Karenni National People's Party in the fight for the independence of the Kayah State of Myanmar/Burma, where the Padaung came from. The people of this village make a decent wage from tourist money and live much better than if they lived in Myanmar, working at hard labor all day.

The hill tribes of Thailand, including the Padaung, face many hardships. The Padaung are treated as refugees, not Thai citizens. Without basic rights as Thai citizens, the Padaung have no access to education, jobs, medical care, or land ownership. The Thai government allows these people to stay because of their value to tourism.

The Padaung used to have a sustainable lifestyle and were able to make available to their people everything they needed from what nature provided.

They made their own clothing, grew their own food, and traded for other necessary items. They made cups, lanterns, water buckets, dishes, and spoons from bamboo.

The villagers now use modern metal pots for cooking and plastic buckets for carrying water. They eat with their fingers out of metal bowls and drink from metal or plastic cups.

About the Author

Jackie Chase, winner of the Royal Palm Literary Award, has lived temporarily among primitive peoples in many parts of the world and traveled to over 100 countries. She writes this series about children to highlight the world's diversity of customs while at the same time showing how life itself is so similar the world over that we should celebrate the differences and appreciate our common needs for food clothing and shelter, and our children's further desires for recreation, toys and learning.

See her blog at:

WorldTravelDiva.com for her list of books. Please write to share YOUR story with her.

Image	Photo List	Image	Photo List
1	BKK260-0A Mucha playing hand games	26	BKK 00-87 Washing clothes at the well
2	BKK 00-66 Teenage giraffe-neck girl	27	BKK 100-1A Three-year-old washing her own clothing
3	BKK 100-6A Typical village hut		
4	BKK 260-24A Winding fabric to wear under harsh metal rings	28	BKK 60-19A Mucha's mom washing clothes in buckets
5	BKK 00-82 Mucha's house	29	BKK 00-68 Mucha's bath time at the well
6	BKK 250-12A Young Karen tribal girl	30	BKK 4 Friends scrubbing neck rings at bath time
7	BKK 1 Catching locusts with bamboo pole	31	BKK 3-6 Scrubbing brass rings
8	BKK 70-6 Playing with locust before eating it raw	32	BKK 5 Mucha's family
		33	BKK 6 Sleeping with rings
9	BKK 2 Playing hopscotch	34	BKK 00-92 Children playing
10	BKK 27-20 Jump rope with rubber bands tied into rope	35	BKK 7 Babysitting baby brother
		36	BKK 260-15A Snack time for Mucha and her brothers
11	BKK 00-80 Back strap weaving		
12	BKK 60-12A Mucha making pretend mud pies	37	BKK 240-12A Stained teeth from chewing betel nuts
13	BKK 00-78 Boys in school classroom	38	BKK 00-82 Ma' Da in her house
14	BKK 100-14A Watching neighbors play from window	39	BKK 270-15 Ma' Da is Mucha's teenage friend
15	BKK 00-85 Girls in classroom	40	BKK 100-16A Trying to sell jewelry
16	BKK 00-77 Roasting a pig over a fire	41	BKK 2-3 Four-year-old carving bamboo with knife
17	BKK 00-91 Carrying a cooked pig		
18	BKK 00-69 Mucha choosing a duck for dinner	42	BKK 100-20A Weaving on a back-strap loom
19	BKK 250-22A Showing ducks to Mucha	43	BKK 70-23 Padaung mother shading her baby
20	BKK 270 -10 Mucha's father building a cement walkway	44	BKK 8 Karen woman buying snacks from girls
21	BKK 3 Cutting bamboo	45	BKK 70-18 Five-year-old long neck girl
22	BKK 00-61 Stitching handles on bag	46	BKK 00-50 Typical village home
23	BKK 250-15A Padaung man selling bow and arrow	47	BKK 250-10A Author with long-neck child
24	BKK 50-2 Cooling off at the well before dinner		
25	BKK 9 Naptime		

www.ingramcontent.com/pod-product-compliance
Lightning Source LLC
Chambersburg PA
CBHW060556100426
42742CB00013B/2584